PS.ARCHIVE

Vol - 2

"For to be idle is to become a stranger unto seasons, and to set up life's procession that marches in majesty and proud submission to the infinite."

-Khalil Gibran

INDEX

PROLOGUE

In the most advanced days of Kali Yug,
When easy, lazy lives are blessed by the hard work of
lunatics,
In a world where democracy has won, but labor still
sledgehammers the soul,
Where fame is a prized possession,
When sins are treasured as gold,
And everyone is a Gemini—a wounded rich man and a
corrupt cynic.

Amidst this, there was born a true Gemini—
A beautiful woman, with eyes carrying the life the world had
lost,
Lips like roads to heaven,
Her words precisely expressing a devotee's vision and plea,
And thoughts, always in pursuit of the profound, and beyond.

She enjoyed the comfortable life the Modern Age had gifted
her,
Yet struggled to keep pace with the blind labyrinth.
The labyrinth where:
Purpose is equated to God,
God is equated to Religion,
Religion is equated to Politics,
Politics is equated to Business,
And Business is equated to a One-Man Deal—
A One Man who may not be the Purpose hoped for.

Rather:
Purpose has become self-sufficient,
God, a therapist,
Religion, the disharmony of unison,
Politics, service for the competent,

Business, purposeless,
And the One-Man Deal, the hollow self.

To escape this circus for a while, she sits by the ocean,
camouflaged among the glittering sand grains,
Frying herself in spiraling thoughts under the sun.
She asked the ocean,
"Oh dear Love,

I made a mistake, had a lapse, regretted it, accepted it, and
changed for the better.

I hoped the dimension of my life would change overall. I
hoped to see the dawn. I hoped I'd feel out of the darkness
and sharp coldness.

And, I made a mistake again. My run around the world, the
sphere never ended.

I rested, and depended on many, all for scaring them away.
Every day feels like a struggle, every place a war zone, and
everyone is too distant and disconnected.
Permanence is nowhere to be found.

Everything—opportunities, feelings, people, and
moments—feels disdained.
The feeling of belonging is unknown."

The silence, the echoes of the waves, the beam of light,
Became the silence in her, the echoes of her undulting mind,
and her answers.

Meaning *(Artha)*

The Weight of Gold

Gold,
Is all I ever wanted.
But when granted,
And when I had a hold,
It felt like a burden,
All of a sudden.

Gold, and bars of silver—
They gleamed, they shone, my only way.
At least, it was what
I truly thought.

Gold, and some pieces of solitaires,
Felt like the need of the hour.
They were treasures I'd kill for,
I wanted to have it all and be a giver.
I longed for the power
To keep others under,
And to nurture as their mother.

Gold,
And the weight of it,
 Dragged me into a pit,
Where I found the mold
Of the crown
That everyone wore with a frown.

Gold, and all the cash,
The keys,
To endless pleas.
The taste of wealth,
Crept in with stealth.

Gold, and the villain in me,
Made me want more, endlessly.
Now my body is sore.
Taller the ladder,
The lonelier and sadder.
The thirst, the hunger,
Consumes me like thunder.

The Value of the Void

There's a heart behind this face.
There's a face behind this mask.
There's a mask behind this mind.
I see my face, and nothing else.
I dare not to ask
If I could ever not fake what is at the hind.

"What do I see there?"
I needed to quit everywhere,
To learn the value of the void,
To let the heart and mind colloid.

There's passion behind identity.
There's identity behind persona.
There's a persona behind duty.
I try to lose the intensity
And cleanse my aura,
And settle for serenity.

"What do I feel in myself?"
I needed to kill the hungry wolf,
To learn the value of the void,
To let the passion and duty colloid.

There's love behind intuition.
There's intuition behind vulnerability.
There's vulnerability behind a bond.
I try to give it all when I'm slippin',
And I had to admit my inability
To love with no bound.

"What is the ultimate need?"
I had to take the lead,

To learn the value of the void,
To let love and bond collide.

The Eternal Exchange

I wonder how to let go;
Sometimes, I ought to throw.
But that's alright—
At least it feels like I'm living
For the first time in a million nights.

I wish I could tell my old self
That everything is brighter on the same side,
That I have no need to hide
From my true self,
And that people around me take me into the sea like a warm
tide.

I wonder how to keep
My authentic self that always weeps,
To look at the bright light.
At least the tears are what I'm sieving
For the last time in a million nights.

I wish I could tell my future self
To remember the path that I came awhile,
That taught me the value of a silly smile,
And all the parallels
That helps me preserve my hyle.

It is the eternal exchange—
Change is the only permanence.
But all I do is breathe and change,
To be better, despite the turbulence.

I strive to be grateful
To the universe and the angels,
For I, being able to read in reverse,
And for me to be seeing
The boon in every curse.

I wish I could tell myself,
Every morning, my prayers and gratitude
Have purified my crude,
Defeated my Relf,
And blessed my virtue.

Righteousness *(Dharma)*

The Path Unknown

When duty aligns with the soul's purpose.
When you see the beauty of life
When you are away from all the chaos
When you breathe and feel the high

You know,
All your mistakes were to align you on your track.
You feel,
All the warmth after the snow storm.
You see,
All the beautiful memories in your trash shaft.

When you enjoy every meal, every day
When you smile at puppies, sky and the moon
When you laugh at silly jokes your maid says
When you cry watching a rising sun

You know,
All the misunderstood love blossoms to its clarity
You feel,
All the calmness behind your boisterous heart
You see,
All the light through the window bars

That's when you want to walk out of your room
When you want to quit your comfort zone
When you have enough to watch a flower bloom
When you take the path unknown

You know,
For once, that everything is alright

You feel,
For once, that you forever be at peace
You see,
For once and for all where you belong

Mirror To The Self

I stood between the dessert and the ocean,
Presuming it to be a rough patch.
Little did I know I'd be a golden membrane
That would help me unlock the latch.

I saw,
How truth reveals the essence of responsibility,
How stillness let me see with lucidity,
How alive I was,
And how unaware I was.

I saw,
How love reveals the essence of compassion,
How feeling sorry and forgiving isn't just an action,
But through that road seemed endless
Until I became a mirror to the self.

My friends saw a clear change.
Everyday, I write a new page.
I embrace everything that is on my way.
I see a new day everyday.

I saw,
How relationships rekindle and resonate,
How all the dots finally connect,
How the climax never ends anymore,
And how I want more of this for evermore.

Harmony In Chaos

Finding righteousness amidst moral dilemmas,
But I'm afraid to step further
And see what the next chapter holds for me,
See whatever life holds for me.

Seeking balance in the turbulence of life,
I've loved every step of this way,
But who knows the next leap?
Who knows what is the next leap?

I swam across the deep sea
To be at the golden bridge.
Let me be,
At least let me feel.

Unveiling serenity in the fragrance of the amethyst,
But I'm afraid of the next rot.
Also I'm curious about the next garden
And who awaits my pardon.

Deciphering truths in the shuffle of the tarot cards,
A delicate trial of faith and fate.
What do they tell me?
Should I let them be?

I swam across the deep sea
To be at the golden bridge.
Let me be,
At least let me feel.

Chasing freedom in the whispers of the unknown,
I'm afraid gave up on everything

That the world fought for,
That the world fought a war for.

But I swam across a deep sea,
A horrendous ride of life and death,
To be at the golden bridge-
A place when I found pieces of myself.

Let me be,
At least let me feel
Free.

Desires *(Kama)*

The Dance of Longing

I've waited a while,
For you.
With a bright smile,
I swam through
A million miles,
Just for you.

I sat there as a replacement
Of you.
At a round table, giving two cents,
I talked through
My resentment,
 Just for you.

Turning yearning into celebration,
The dance of longing that melts devastation.
"Don't let yourself keep him,"
 I say that whenever it gets dim.

Without you,
With you,
The hiraeth
Feels so true.

I sit by the shore
In search of you.
I jumped into my core,
In the deepest, darkest blue.
I open the magic shop door
To find me in you.

Turning longing into a waltz with the moon,
I keep dancing with myself, and maybe you.

There is no harm in this wait,
Except that I have to tighten my gut.

Without you,
With you,
The hiraeth
Feels so true.

The Fire Within

I can't fight this anymore.
I've tried my best to keep the fire alive.
I keep charging my heart to survive,
Before it rots on the shore.

I fear becoming a bore.
I pretend to be natural, but I contrive.
I relentlessly attempt to be compassionate, but I have to revive,
Because I keep to myself whatever is bitter.

Harnessing passion to fuel creativity and love,
I search for the spark in everyone,
In every eye, and in every heart.

Channeling my fire to touch the mystic power above,
I search for the God in everyone,
In every eye, and in every heart.

Some are deeply intimidated
By love, trust, and faith.
They sing the seven notes, and I hear the eighth.
They presume I am delusional and sedated.

I surrender to be illuminated
In the light of the morning sun that gave me a bath,
Cleansing the darkness and the wraith,
Giving me a license to be passionate.

Igniting the soul every time I want to forego and grow,
I search for reason in everyone,
In every eye, and in every heart.

Chasing the flame, the light, and the glow,
I search for passion in everyone,
In every eye, and in every heart.

Beyond the Chase

Where fulfillment replaces pursuit,
Where all our questions are answered,
Where it is always alright to give up,
Where time flies by in a blink of an eye,
That is where we belong.
That is where we bury our song.

Where everything seems to be out of place,
Where you feel uneasy every once in a while.
I was chasing a home,
I was tailgating others' homes,
I couldn't settle,
Until I understood that I can't be brittle,
Except for in my home.

Where food is served hot,
Where I don't have to worry about laundry,
Where people are concerned for me,
And I don't have to in return.
That is where I belong,
To comprehend that I took too long.

This giant place
Is my home, and I was in denial.
We are blessed children,
Who are impulsive
And act repulsive,
'Cause of our need to be free like a wren.

What lies beyond the chase?
Have we ever asked ourselves?
There lies another chase,
Until we tone down our pace.

We don't understand
That we are here on this land,
To not live on a strand,
But by a command.

Liberation *(Moksha)*

The Art of Letting Go

"Don't let me have you."
How easy is it to say that?
"Do you even think about me?"
How difficult is it to ask that?

What makes it worthy of the stay?
What makes it worthless to throw?
What makes it so consuming?
What makes the coastline devastating?

Freedom begins with surrender.
I let myself leave from the spell I was under
By tossing your thoughts in the sea.
I await your gunshot to flee.

"Do I burn the notes named after you?"
How easy of a task is that?
"Did you learn about my feathers spree?"
And ask me, how hard was that?

What makes it worth the wait?
What makes the effort futile?
What makes me want to devour the moment?
What brings apathy to the same moment?

Acceptance is the gateway to inner peace.
I let myself know thyself
By lobbing memories in the air,
For them to find their way back to me.

It was so easy to watch it all go
It was the best decision ever
To let things go with the flow

And watch the bloom of my afterglow
I held too tight, afraid to fall,
Yet love was never mine to own.
The tides would rise, the tides would call,
And still, I stood there all alone.
The winds will take what's meant to stray,
No hands can cage a fleeting soul,
So I embrace the art of letting go.

The Silent Horizon

Peace found in the stillness of the present.
In the silent, empty streets
Of my village, bent,
Which completes
The wide smile that greets.

Stopping the world to unravel what's within,
In the presumed cage,
Where my life began,
Where I set the stage
To replay the conceived rampage.

Pausing life's rush,
Seeking silence to understand the self,
Resuming life for a push,
And coming back in stealth
To the silent horizon.
And meditate with Siddhartha
Until I found the reason,
And dance again to my passionate flaws.

Flight back home with the wings of renewal,
I call it the rebirth,
As I gave up the dual, rule, and jewel,
To fill my heart with mirth,
And all the love on this Earth.

Journey through the skies, with freedom as my guide,
I compelled the stars to follow,
And the moon to take me as its bride,
To dance with me when it's mellow,
To have a laughter of our own, bellow.

The Infinite Within

In search of a little drop of light,
I wandered the world,
With my eyes blinded by the weight
Of the shape I'm expected to mold.

Living fully as the gateway to eternity,
Overflowing with love
And misery at the same time, in verity,
Hoping for a cure from up above.

The happiness in making memories,
The bitterness in wrecking bonds,
The rage in the war for glory,
The serenity in trusting the beyond.

The infinite within,
The absolute one within.

In hunt of a little hope,
I confided in many arms,
And chose to slide down a slope,
Only to wake up to the world's alarms.

Embracing now, the path to the One and Infinity,
Waiting in the wings,
At the front door of divinity,
Struggling to give up the kings, rings, and strings.

The fear of going back to square one,
The amusement in starting afresh,
The faith in the universe,
The wait while hoping for love.

The infinite within,
The absolute one within.

Nature *(Prakriti)*

The Ultimatum

Winds of Belonging

I stand there alone,
In the wind, under a tree,
Waging my life to nature, that's overgrown,
Hoping it would give me comfort and peace.

I stand amongst paintings
Of the biggest artist of the nation,
Adding a golden plating
To the rustic bridge where I took a station.

Finding your place within the universe,
Hoping to write a better verse,
I see the miracles—
Per se, I feel free from the curse.

I stand there in a crowd,
Waiting for a sign,
Screaming my heart out,
Begging for a reason to have faith.

My path in the vastness of the cosmos,
Feeling the winds of belonging,
Lying on the greenest grass,
Raining the pathetic pathos.

It is the breeze,
It is the wind,
It is the storm,
It is a tornado.

But it is our breath,
It is our only faith.

The Ocean's Whisper

I sit on the shore,
Hoping to have a reciprocal disclosure.
The waves struggle to reach my feet.
I accept my defeat.
I say, "I go first,"
And I blurt,
Hoping the moulvis
Would clear the carps and calvis.

Lessons of resilience from nature's vastness,
I tossed a pebble into the deep darkness.

I see a bright glint,
And that is when I started to print.
I still sat there,
To see the subtle smile of the wave bearer.
Sometimes I camouflage,
Just to self-sabotage.
At the end of tracks,
I'd be crouched to death in the climax.

The fear of mundane existence,
The fear of me becoming the actor of actors,
The fear of me decepting my persistence.
In the ocean's whispers.

I struggle to keep it alive with the sea.
It gets very lonely.
But now and then I go back to the shore
Hoping for a prophet to show up.

Roots and Wings

Roots and wings,
Snow storms and springs—
Which one do I settle for?
Fire and mire,
Aversion and desire—
Which one do I settle for?

Strength lies in knowing when to stay and when to soar.
I've tried my best to shut the door.
I also tried to welcome an ugly boar.
Between sweet and bitter, I am stuck at sour,
Because I want them both,
I deserve both.
I belong here and there.
In sweet and bitter,
There are blue ocean waves that call me in.
There is a red dessert that fills me from within.

The lightness in the weight is when you know,
When to hold and when to let go.
I needed the final aspect
Before I deject everything I thought was perfect.
The impotence in the power is when you know,
When to hold your ground and when to rise above.
I blamed the sky and my fate,
Until I understood what it could create.

Because I want them both,
I deserve both.
I belong here and there.
In sweet and bitter,
There are blue ocean waves that call me in.
There is a red dessert that fills me from within.

In the blue sea, I see the false me.
In the red dessert, I see what I avert.
In the green garden,
Where I don't play pretend,
In the orange morning sky,
Where I merrily fly.
In the indigo morning glory,
Where I narrate my story.

The cowardice of courage is when you know,
When to retreat and embrace the storm.
I stand by my insecurity
To win over prosperity.

Time *(Kala)*

The Pulse of Eternity

I drive to the past,
Stations surpassed.
Every moment
Holds the infinite
That brought me here,
From where I see clear—
A vision I cheer for.

I see them leaving,
That's what time does,
Conceiving, dismissing
The memories of us.

I urge toward the future,
So many stops ahead.
What could be my next enclosure?
I wish to clear the cloud
And glimpse what time holds:
The eternity pulse,
Or the fleeting hush.

I see them coming,
People I've dreamt of,
Humming, drumming,
Sweeping me off.

And what's in between,
What goes unseen,
The golden scene
That lives evergreen.

What's the present?
The infinite current,

Gazillion moments
That is just left.

Sands of Wisdom

The sand clock in your shelf,
I watch it all the time.
Now that you left me to myself,
I think of you and lose track of time.

What does time teach those who listen?
Is it the birth of a memory?
Is it the death of a moment?
I seek sands of wisdom.

I've been still for a whole year.
Time passed by me,
Trying to understand what I fear—
Something I managed to see.

What does time facilitate for those who participate?
Is it living a cherishable memory?
Is it killing a detestable moment?
I seek sands of wisdom.

All my life,
I have been drifting like the sand.
And now I'm empty on the top.

I waited,
All that I could,
Before I was ready to invert
And start cascading again.

The Timeless Dance

I look back to our pictures,
And giggle like a baby.
Some memories never rupture,
As I let them devour me.

I become five again;
I sit in your lap.
The furniture still remains—
All that has changed is the gap

Between you and me.
I still believe your existence,
Though, in the sky, I see thee.
I embrace life's rhythm without resistance.

I dance through my sorrow;
I sing along the unhappy sparrows.
I have been with myself
In every ball—my timeless dance.

I become twenty again;
I stand beside your coffin.
For love, I bargained—
Until I learned love is from within.

A politician said, "Acceptance is life."
It took half a decade to understand,
Until I watched a lone star play a fife,
And I stood there to watch him on a barren land.

I dance through my pain;
I sing along the seven sisters.

I have been with myself
In every ball—my timeless dance.

Faith *(Shraddha)*

The Courage to Trust

I detested the God,
Per se, the Universe.
I looked for a fraud
In every coerce.

Faith was the first step on my unseen path.
Either way led to death,
But what's valued is the life
And the perth
That is in between the birth and wrath,
That is between mistrust and faith.

That took me places
Where I was destined to be.
The toughest phases,
Where I understood the real 'me.'

The seasons might change,
The world may declutter.
I would have to outrange
Beyond my world for the better.

The moment I spoke his name,
All the stars below turned crimson.
I jumped in excitement,
I bawled in glisten.
I saw the red string attachment
That is between you and me,
That is between destiny and reality.

That took me decisions
Which I had to partake,

The toughest choices,
Where I had the courage to trust.

Beyond Blindness

How do we see what lies beyond?
Every inevitable incident,
Is it one of the gazillion cascading moments,
Or is it the moment that we lived all our life for?

When belief is rooted in understanding,
That life is merely trying our best to just breathe,
There come many distractions—
The need, want, and desire to be upstanding.

We are mere mortals,
Structured to make need a greed.
We are mere animals,
Wired to hunt and eat.

Every moment is born with a problem of its own,
And we get carried away by the loan,
So as to forget "the why?"
And "the what?"

Why do we have to rush through a flume?
Why do we have to search for a lume?
What blinds in this hunt?
What lies beyond blindness?

The Light Within

There is something about stillness,
Something calm,
And something wondrous,
Like a deer away from wolves.
I feel light, with no predator nor prey,
Illuminating the journey through inner trust.
I wake up to the light from my window crux;
Everything has been alright,
Since I patiently waited for it to set in light.

There is something about the change,
Something warm,
And something strange,
Like a cinematic montage.
I feel sharp, with no image or mirage,
Guiding the path with unwavering faith.
I'm ready to fall down again with grace,
Everything has been sound and bright,
Since I patiently waited for it to set in light.

I am well aware
That I have to beware
Of the next fall pit
That is going to bring the dark bit.
But I have seen
The light within.

Urgency *(Samvega)*

The Sharp Awakening

Spending about half a decade
In a place unknown,
With people who completely belonged.
I had to prepare for a farewell from day one.
Clarity found in the haste of passing moments.,
I had to plan everything ahead:
The words that would write on my own eulogy
And the flowers on my coffin head.

Spending about six months
As a judged hostile,
With people who are ambitious,
I had to prepare for my next mystery move.
Insight found in the fleeting moments of now.
When a friend of mine said,
"It is what it is,"
I knew I had to admit fall pits and raids.

I am where I always wanted to be,
In a golden rim.
But, this is weary,
To settle and not swim.
Something has to keep us going:
A next target,
A fast-paced ladder is growing,
For us to sweat.

Discovery in the passing seconds of today,
When I lay back in my home
That I have to leave behind,
In order to keep moving.

The Compass of Priorities

Traversing in all wrong directions,
Map hidden in my pocket,
I learned the need to be lost.
Well, it is to be found,

Learning to focus on what truly matters.
I lost track of time in the nothingness—
Of being monotonous,
Of writing the same thing,
Of thinking back at the same moment.

I had to go wild,
Throw the compass of priorities,
And pack my bags to go with the wind.
But I do have my liabilities.

The setbacks don't keep me back anymore;
They are just there, and still let me wander.
I created my headspace
To handle shit at its pace.
It is a must to learn the layers.

I wanted to be there,
Everywhere I was destined to go.
They said, "Never say never."
"You gotta do what you gotta do."

To just be there
Was all I had to do—
To throw the compass
And be lost of directions.

Breath of Resolve

It cost me four years of fair fight
To learn that I can never win or lose
Against time, against might.
All I had to do was cruise,

Finding calm even in the race against time.
I did that by taking a pit stop.
For once and for all,
I let time go by.
I watch it go by.
I feel it go by.

I look around, and I know—
I lived this moment.
So, as to know this,
I had to lose the races and wars.
They weren't losses;
They were mere stairs,
Guiding me into solace.

I had to take that breath to resolve,
To understand the puzzle—
A puzzle never solved,
Only experienced,
Lived through,
And remembered.

Joy (Ananda)

Fragments of Bliss

We sat there together
On a fine night,
When your husband
And my best friend
Were tied to seats,
Playing something silly,

Discovering happiness in life's small moments.
When you and I gathered all my fragments,
I would remember that with you.
The night on the couch—when I knew
I'd gathered moments of bliss.
Someone will do yours.

We sat there together
On a planetarium swing.
The sight of little children
Took away all the burden.
We were far away,
But these memories, we relay.

We sat there together
On the terrace of your apartment,
Watching the lake
And the stars that were just awake.
You've loved all my facets,
And you've undone all my facades,

Embracing the quiet beauty of everyday life.
When I learned to put myself together,
I would remember that with you.
That night beside the lake—I knew

I'd gathered moments of bliss.
Someone will do yours.

Life is all about these
Fragments of bliss
That someone puts together.
Our ultimate purpose is to gather
Tiny pieces of us—
To make somebody else's
Fragments of bliss.

The Glow of Kindness

My melanin-rich skin
Shines like gold under the sun,
Like never before,
Like never better.

I resemble my grandmother
In the eyes of the oldies in my foyer.
I've undone my sins,
I float like a fish with no fins.

I feel light as a feather
After the hither-thither.
How joy multiplies through giving!
I just had to be kind to make a living.
The money I earned
Was good enough for my rent,
But nothing could steal my smile.
I dared the world to throw me a rile.

I cried often on my bed;
My pillow was my only bud.
But the next day, I wake up to
Another day of hiding my blue.
The real happiness blossomed
When I make someone feel fathomed.

There is a thin line between
Selfishness and self-compassion.
To be the latter
Does not mean you can't aim high on your ladder.

The Unveiled Smile

Roots
The tangled roots,
At the mangrove forest,
Where I mourn all my losses.
In the boat again,
I think about what I was then.

Water
I put my legs in the water,
To recollect all our laughter,
And to worry about what comes after,
After you, and after us.
Life, death, and thus.

Finding joy in self-discovery,
Finding joy in solitary,
Finding joy in the wind gush,
Finding joy in the slowed rush.

Row
I tell the boatman to row,
Until we reach the deep low.
All my sadness, I throw,
To let myself free,
And happily flee.

Finding joy in the busy night,
Finding joy in the beam of light,
Finding joy in the endless sky,
Finding joy in the unveiled smile.

Essence *(Rasa)*

Shades of the Soul

You make your way through the sea
That I was watching for decades now,
And at once, when all my dreams come to me,
I don't know how to accept and allow.

Every experience is a hue of the masterpiece
That your master painted, only to smudge.
To see my life unfold at ease,
I should've learned to interpret all at once.
Nobody feels at ease
Until they paint shades of their soul—

The blues in the trust,
The red in the love,
The gold in the bond,
The art in the soul.

I waited my way through the sea
That you were crossing for decades now,
And at once, when all the doors are closed,
I feel small and imposed.

Every moment is a brushstroke on the canvas
Of our story, framed in glass.
To see you find me
On your way makes me weightless.
Nobody feels at easeUntil they paint shades of their soul—

The blues in the misery,
The red in rage,
The golden in us,
The art of sticking around,

Despite not feeling at ease,
Until we paint shades of our soul.

The Art of Living

Karma digs me in,
And holds my hand to come up again.
I try again and again,
To not bargain
With God to offer me something
In exchange for my devotion.
I feel ashamed after begging,
To give me conviction,

To feel like the one in a crowd,
To feel like one in the crowd.
Existence as both creation and creator,
Existence as both prey and predator.
I learn the art of life.

Destiny scares me,
By pushing me from a spiral spree,
Just to let me free,
Have a happy flea,
But to pay its fee,
For the job and the degree,
That I do and don't fancy.
It keeps me on my knees in a constant plea,

To swim in a deep blue sea,
To sit at the shore, lost in the waves' endless plea.
Life's a puzzle, with pieces yet to fit.
I embrace with love the words of the prophet.
In every lesson, I find the art of life.

The Symphony Within

I've loved you for a lifetime.
It's more like it is fictional.
I'm not sure who is at fault.
I weighed all my faith on time.
You and I are conditional.
All the "if onlys" determine our result.

When life resonates with the heart's essence,
You feel the pull of fate in your limbs.
You start to slow dance
To the symphony from within.

When the soul aligns with the rhythm of the universe,
You feel the higher power in your bones.
You start to slow dance
To the symphony from within.

I believe in the divine will,
The red thread of fate,
That binds us.
When there is a will,
There is a way,
Regardless of the paths
That you and I choose.

When the spirit dances with the breeze of destiny,
You feel the threads of our past tangled.
You start to slow dance
To the symphony from within.

We never danced under the rain,
We never grooved beside the sea,

We never swayed along the wind,
But we always did the symphony from within.